D1394669

Rainbows

THROUGH THE RAIN

FIONA CASTLE

Rainbows
THROUGH THE RAIN

Hodder & Stoughton
LONDON SYDNEY AUCKLAND

British Library Cataloguing in Publication Data
A record for this book is available from
the British Library

ISBN 0-340-70980-4

Printed and bound in Great Britain by
Clays Ltd, St Ives plc

Hodder and Stoughton Ltd
A division of Hodder Headline PLC
338 Euston Road
London NW1 3BH

Contents

***

Acknowledgments

✳ ✳ ✳

While every effort has been made to contact the copyright holders of material used in this book, this has not always been successful. Full acknowledgment will gladly be made in future editions.

We gratefully acknowledge the following, extracts from which appear in this book:

Amy Carmichael, *Rose from Bier*, copyright © 1933, The Dohnavur Fellowship, published by Christian Literature Crusade, Fort Washington, PA, USA. Used by permission.

Dr James Dobson, *When God Doesn't Make Sense* (adapted), © Tyndale House Publishers Inc. Used by permission. All rights reserved.

Elizabeth Elliot, *Love has a Price Tag*, HarperCollins Ltd.

Elizabeth Elliot, *A Path through Suffering*, Paternoster Publishing.

Stephen Gaukroger, *It Makes Sense*, © Stephen Gaukroger, published by Scripture Union.

Jim Graham, *Dying to Live*. Used by permission of the author.

Oscar Hammerstein, 'You'll never walk alone'. Permission granted by IMP Ltd, Essex, UK.

W. Philip Keller, *A Shepherd Looks at the 23rd Psalm*, copyright © 1970. Used by permission of Zondervan Publishing House.

Brian Doerkson, 'Faithful One', copyright © 1989
    Mercy/Vineyard Publishing, administered by
    CopyCare, PO Box 77, Hailsham, BN27 3EF
    UK. Used by permission.

Robert Frost, 'Road not Taken', taken from *The
    Poetry of Robert Frost*, edited by Edward Connery
    and published by Jonathan Cape. Used by
    permission. With thanks to the estate of Robert
    Frost.

Graham Kendrick, 'Come and See', copyright ©
    Makeway Music, PO Box 263, Croydon, Surrey,
    CR9 5AP. International copyright secure. Used by
    permission. All rights reserved.   .

Ulrich Shaeffer, 'Into Your Light'. Used by
    permission of HarperCollins Ltd.

Shirley Vickers, 'Damaged Goods – Return to
    Maker', written in 1996 while undergoing radio
    and chemotherapy treatment

Tommy Walker, 'He Turned my Mourning into
    Dancing', © 1992. Integrity's Hosanna Music, by
    Kingsway Thankyou music.

John Wimber, 'O Let the Son of God Enfold You'.
    copyright © 1989 Mercy/Vineyard Publishing,
    administered by CopyCare, PO Box 77, Hailsham,
    BN27 3EF UK. Used by permission.

RAINBOWS THROUGH THE RAIN

*D*uring a time of shock or pain or grief, it is often *difficult* to concentrate on anything for any length of time – as I discovered when my husband, Roy Castle, died after two and a half years battling with cancer – and reading a book would be out of the question. I have therefore compiled a few poems and thoughts and verses which have helped and encouraged me through some bleak times and enabled me to have a thankful rather than despairing heart.

As with any literature, tastes are deeply personal and some pieces which others had found helpful I did not.

I hope that through these pages, some of these thoughts will bring hope and encouragement to your own heart.

O LOVE THAT WILT NOT
LET ME GO

O Love that wilt not let me go
I rest my weary soul in thee;
I give thee back the life I owe,
That in thine ocean depths its flow
May richer, fuller be.

O Light that followest all my way,
I yield my flickering torch to thee;
My heart restores its borrowed ray,
That in thy sunshine's blaze its day
May brighter, fairer be.

O Joy that seekest me through pain,
I cannot close my heart to thee;
I trace the rainbow through the rain,
And feel the promise is not vain
That morn shall tearless be.

O Cross that liftest up my head,
I dare not ask to fly from thee;
I lay in dust life's glory dead,
And from the ground there blossoms red
Life that shall endless be.

George Matheson

PART ONE

Love

***

O Love that wilt not let me go,
I rest my weary soul in thee;
I give thee back the life I owe,
That in thine ocean depths its flow
May richer, fuller be.

God has not promised skies always blue,
flower-strewn pathways all our lives through;
God has not promised sun without rain,
Joy without sorrow, peace without pain.

God has not promised smooth roads and wide
swift easy travel heeding no guide;
God has not promised that we shall not bear
many a burden, many a care.

But God has promised strength for the day,
rest for the labour, light for the way,
Grace for the trials, help from above
unfailing sympathy, undying love.

Annie Johnson Flint

I will not forget you ... I have held you in
the palm of my hand.

Isaiah 49:15–16

There is a beautiful sculpture of a small child laying his head into the cupped hand of the Lord. What a beautiful picture of the Father's love for His children. It became very special to me when my older daughter went to a far flung part of the world for the first time. As I prayed for her I heard the Lord whisper to me, 'Don't worry about Julia, I have her in the palm of My hand.' I don't worry about her, I pray that she will always remain in that secure place, wherever He sends her.

Don't worry about anything; instead pray about everything; tell God your needs and don't forget to thank Him for His answers. If you do this you will experience God's peace which is far more wonderful than the human mind can understand. His peace will keep your thoughts and your hearts quiet and at rest as you trust in Christ Jesus.

Philippians 4:6–7

Lord, more and more
I pray Thee, or by wind or fire,
Make pure my inmost heart's desire
And purge the clinging chaff from off the floor.

I wish Thy way.
But when in me myself would rise
And long for something otherwise,
Then, Holy One, take sword and spear and slay.

Oh, stay near by,
Most patient Love, till, by Thy grace,
In this poor silver, Thy bright face
Shows forth in clearness and serenity.

What will it be
When, like the lily or the rose,
That in Thy flowery garden
I shall be flawless, perfect, Lord, to Thee?

Amy Carmichael

This next poem was sent to me after my son, Daniel, aged fifteen, had nearly died falling from a cliff. It was a very traumatic time for all of us and these words were a great comfort.

He giveth more grace when burdens grow greater
He sendeth more strength when the labours increase
To added afflictions He addeth His mercies
To multiplied trials His multiplied peace.

When we have exhausted our store of endurance
When our strength has failed ere the day is half done,
When we reach the end of our hoarded resources
Our Father's full giving is only begun.

His love has no limit, His grace has no measure
His power no boundary known unto men
For out of His infinite riches in Jesus
He giveth and giveth and giveth again.

Annie Johnson Flint

*S*ent to me by a thoughtful person on Roy's death.

We seem to give them back to Thee, O God, who gavest them to us. Yet as Thou didst not lose them in giving, so we do not lose them by their return. Not as the world giveth, givest Thou, O Lover of souls. What Thou givest, Thou takest not away, for what is Thine is ours also if we are Thine. And life is eternal and love is immortal, and death is only an horizon, and an horizon is nothing save the limit of our sight. Lift us up, strong Son of God, that we may see further; cleanse our eyes that we may see more clearly: draw us closer to Thyself that we may know ourselves to be nearer to our loved ones who are with Thee. And while Thou dost prepare a place for us, prepare us also for that happy place, that where Thou art we may be also for evermore.

Bishop Brent

Let not your heart be troubled. You are trusting God, now trust in Me. There are many homes up there where my Father lives, and I am going to prepare them for your coming. When everything is ready then I will come and get you so that you can always be with Me where I am.

John 14:1–3

You do not know what will happen to-morrow. For what is your life? It is even a vapour that appears for a little time and then vanishes away.

James 4:14

We have such a few years to do the things the Lord wants each of us to do. To miss that is to miss everything. I think that's what James felt when he went on to say, 'For what is your life? It is even a vapour that appears for a little time and then vanishes away' (4:14). The image is of the morning mists or fog that hovers around the peak of a mountain and then dissolves as the sun rises and the winds blow.

Life is like that. Our purpose is to know, love, and glorify the Lord and become prepared to live with Him forever. In the brief span of this life He will guide our thinking and willingness to accomplish His plan for us. I've never known a person to have a nervous breakdown doing what the Lord wills. He never asks us to do more than He is willing to provide strength for us to do. He does not guide us into a burnout. The Spirit of the Lord in us is an eternal flame, and the promise made by John the Baptist is true for us: Christ baptises with fire!

Ten words fan the fire of His Spirit in us. James tells us we are to say, 'If the Lord wills, we shall live and do this or that' (4:15). There's the antidote to burnout, the motto of a beautiful life. Saying those words each hour of every day, in each decision, and in ordering our total life will bring peace and excellence. Success is doing what the Lord wants us to do. He will liberate our wills to implement our total nervous system to carry out what He guides in our thought processes. And He prepares us for decisions that are ahead of us. In consistent times of prayer with Him each day, He gets us ready to make guided choices. When we come up against a decision about which we do not feel sure, it is crucial to put off any choice until we have given Him time to build in us the clarity we need.

Lloyd Ogilvie

*S*usan Lenzkes has an amazing way of getting straight to the heart of the matter with her prose and poems.

I remember, shortly after Roy died, sitting on a train and reading this passage. The tears flowed. I wept tears of pain, of hurt and weariness. The pain of separation was so acute and, in that moment, overwhelming. I recognised my weakness and vulnerability and handed it over to the only One who understood completely how I felt. At that moment I knew I could 'rest' in Him because 'underneath were the Everlasting Arms' (Deuteronomy 33).

The God of all comfort cares for His hurting, weary children. He waits to hear our cry, waits to lift us out of the pit and hold us close to His heart. When He has nourished and strengthened us, then He will teach us how to walk in the calm as well as in the wind.

Susan Lenzkes

*T*he next two poems are from a collection of prose and poems by Shirley Vickers, written whilst undergoing radio and chemotherapy treatment for cancer. She died in 1996, much missed by all who knew her; in my case through Christian Viewpoint.

DAMAGED GOODS
– RETURN TO MAKER

Because I dare to place my feet
   firmly on the stepping stones of God's promises,
I can face this time.

My feelings and powers of logical appraisal
   are all over the place just now,
But when I feel a growing panic –
   I find those early foundations
   on which I built the house of my life
     are still there –
     rock hard and safe.

The undertakings you make
   to those who put their trust in you,
   are just as valid in the unseeing night, as they
     were in the
sunlight when you first showed them to me.

– Because I have changed, you haven't,
Deliver me from doubting this.

Fear and faith make impossible bed-fellows –
  no room for both –
Help my knowledge of your goodness,
  and of your love for me,
  to squeeze out my questions,
    and dispossess my doubting;
  So that whatever comes out of this strangely
      unnerving time,
I can be sure that you will only allow to happen to me
  that which you know I can bear.

Father, into your hands
  I commit myself all over again –
    the family I love,
      the unfinished work I didn't get round to,
        all those unrealised hopes,
          the crying needs of a schizophrenic world,
            and my own helplessness.

Thank you that you go on loving me.

Shirley Vickers

BLACK HOLE
or
A Prayer for those going through dark places

Oh God
    I'm right back in that limbo world again –
      can't feel you close to me –
        can't feel anything.
It seemed as if things were fine –
    walking in the light –
      then suddenly panic: it's all dark:
        I'm drowning.

Worries – no more than there were before –
    and yet they are now so heavy,
      so unsolvable,
        so endless,
          sucking me down –
And I'm listening to the enemy
    who is condemning me to death
      with his sly lies.

Doctors tell us that feeling 'low'
    is just like any other illness –
    brought on by stress, hormones, exhaustion,
      debility,
then why do I feel so guilty about it?
      So powerless to drag myself out?
        So unguarded?

Where is my knowledge of you being there –
  right beside me –
    part of me?
While my feelings scream
  that because I am like this
    I have failed you,
      therefore I am less than nothing –
        useless rubbish?

Please give me the disciplined mind,
  to refuse to entertain these trespassing thoughts –
    which have no right to be there
      because I am your child –.
To wait quietly in faith,
  until my receiving equipment is repaired
    and switched on again
      and I can feel you
        filling me with your big heart,
          forgiving
            empowering
              and re-mobilising me,

      where you have been all the time.

Shirley Vickers

STOP ALL THE CLOCKS

Stop all the clocks, cut off the telephone,
Prevent the dog from barking with a juicy bone,
Silence the pianos and with muffled drum
Bring out the coffin, let the mourners come.

Let aeroplanes circle moaning overhead
Scribbling on the sky the message He Is Dead,
Put crêpe bows round the white necks of the public
    doves,
Let the traffic policemen wear black cotton gloves.

He was my North, my South, my East and West,
My working week and my Sunday rest,
My noon, my midnight, my talk, my song;
I thought that love would last for ever: I was wrong.

The stars are not wanted now: put out every one;
Pack up the moon and dismantle the sun;
Pour away the ocean and sweep up the wood;
For nothing now can ever come to any good.

W. H. Auden

For a short, irrational moment on the day of Roy's death I felt that the world should stop out of respect for his 'passing'. I went into the village and was shocked to discover that everything was going on just as normal, when for me, life, as I had known it, was over.

I'm glad to say that it was momentary and I was

able to laugh at my folly, but Auden's poem sums up my feelings perfectly.

I'm ever more glad that the reality I still hold onto is summed up in the following words from Paul to the Thessalonians:

> And now, dear brothers, I want you to know what happens to a Christian when he dies, so that when it happens, you will not be full of sorrow as those who have no hope.

1 Thessalonians 4:13

FAITHFUL ONE SO UNCHANGING

Faithful One so unchanging;
Ageless One, You're my rock of peace.
Lord of all, I depend on you
I call out to You again and again,
I call out to You again and again.

You are my rock in times of trouble
You lift me up when I fall down
All through the storm
Your love is the anchor
My hope is in You alone.

Brian Doersken

All who listen to my instructions and follow them are wise, like a man who builds his house on solid rock. Though the rain comes in torrents, and the floods rise and the storm winds beat against his house, it won't collapse, for it is built on rock.

But those who hear my instructions and ignore them are foolish, like a man who builds his house on sand. For when the rains and floods come, and storm winds beat against his house, it will fall with a mighty crash.

Matthew 7:24–27

This certain hope of being saved is a strong and trustworthy anchor for our souls, connecting us with God Himself behind the sacred curtain of heaven, where Christ has gone ahead.

Hebrews 6:19

What a foundation you stand on now: the apostles and prophets; and the cornerstone of the building is Jesus Christ himself!

Ephesians 2:20

Look at the birds.
That's what you said, Lord.

And there they are,
just getting on
with the business of living.
Being birds.
Facing the storm.

That's a part of my problem, I reckon.
Not content to be me.
Wanting something different.
Creating my own tensions.
Piling up the building blocks of discontent.
Making my own high-rise apartments of
    unhappiness.
Isolating myself in anxiety.
Made worse
when the hand of reality
gives it all a push,
and I sit,
a child in the ruins,
howling.

Help me understand, Lord,
that wherever I'm at,
you're there.
That you have something for me.
That you care.
As a hen gathers her chicks under her wings,
you said.

Nice picture, that.
Safe from the world,
warm, secure.
But chicks grow up,
and so must I.
Get out into the cold wind
of the world out there.

But knowing that your wings
are stronger than the storm.

I think I can live with that.

Eddie Askew

It isn't the problems that determine our
destiny, it's how we respond.

Anon.

THE GIFT OF TEARS

Who has the wisdom to count the drops of rain
or the tears that flow from heartfelt pain?
As rain comes from the heavens to water the earth,
do tears come from the eyes to water the heart?

It is God who tips over the water jars from the
    heavens.
It is He who put the tears into the soul.
It is He who designed tears to flow from the eyes.
It is He who waters the Spirit to grow in our lives.

So what are tears but a language all of their own
between God the Creator to mankind on earth?
They are the unspoken and unspeakable words of
    wisdom,
our hearts speaking to His heart
and once shared with Him, He is with us.

Joan Morris

I found Joan Morris's poem in Julie Sheldon's The
Blessing of Tears. *Julie wrote this beautiful book as
a result of many tears she herself shed while going
through the trauma of a life-threatening illness. When
God miraculously healed her she spent much time
sharing her story and became very involved with
other people's pain and tears and hence the book was
created.*

Don't be afraid, for the Lord will go before
you; He will not fail nor forsake you.

Deuteronomy 31:8

A rough path is sometimes worth the
treading if, in so doing, we can tread down
the brambles in the path of another.

Anon.

*F*ound in my daily bible reading notes (UCB):

THE BRIDGE BUILDER

An old man going along a highway, came at evening
cold and grey;
To a chasm vast and wide and steep, with waters
rolling cold and deep.
The old man crossed in the twilight dim, the sullen
stream had no fears for him;
But he turned when safe on the other side, and built
a bridge to span the tide.

'Old man,' said a fellow pilgrim near,
'You're wasting your strength with building here;
Your journey will end with the ending day, you never
again will pass this way.
You've crossed the chasm deep and wide, why build
you this bridge at eventide?'
The builder lifted his old grey head, 'Good friend, in
the path I have come,' he said,
'There followeth after me today, a youth whose feet
must pass this way.
The chasm that was as nought to me, to that fair-
haired youth may a pitfall be;
He too must cross in the twilight dim – Good friend,
I'm building this bridge for *him*.'

Will Alan Dromgoole

A CONSOLATION

When in disgrace with fortune and men's eyes
I all alone beweep my outcast state,
And trouble deaf heaven with my bootless cries,
And look upon myself, and curse my fate,
Wishing me like to one more rich in hope,
Featured like him, like him with friends possest,
Desiring this man's art, and that man's scope,
With what I most enjoy contented least;
Yet in these thoughts myself almost despising,
Haply I think on thee – and then my state,
Like to the lark at break of day arising
From sullen earth, sings hymns at heaven's gate;
    For thy sweet love remember'd, such wealth
      brings,
    That then I scorn to change my state with
      kings.

William Shakespeare

arnelle Harris sings this beautiful song on one of his albums. I found it really inspiring on many dark days during Roy's illness.

YOU'RE MY CHILD

As flowers long for sunshine
And as deserts thirst for rain,
That's how much a father longs
To shield his child from pain.
That's not how life happens,
Still I hope that you will see
That I am never far away
For you're a part of me.
You're my child.

You're my child,
And together we can make a dream,
Though tomorrow may seem far away.
You're my child.
Though at times it seems so hard for you to know
Just how far love will go.
Oh it's strong enough to reach across the years,
Through the joys, through the tears,
You're my child.

With words I've said I love you
To express the way I feel,
But the scars can run so deep
That words alone can't heal.
The joy in our tomorrows
Rests in finding Christ today,

And then our happiness is found
Each time we hear him say –

You're my child,
And together we can make a dream.
Though tomorrow may seem far away
You're my child.
Though at times it seems so hard for you to know
Just how far love will go.
Oh it's strong enough to reach across the years,
Through the joys, through the tears,
You're my child.

Larnelle Harris

*T*hrough the grieving process, I have found that different emotions attack me at different times. One evening I was acutely aware of the loss of a loving husband to put his arms around me, hug me and encourage me. I felt so alone ...

The next morning I opened my Living Light (a book of daily bible verses from The Living Bible) and there were the words I needed.

Fear not; you will no longer live in shame. The shame of your youth and the sorrows of widowhood will be remembered no more, for your Creator will be your 'husband'. The Lord of Heaven's armies is His name; He is your redeemer, the Holy One of Israel, the God of all the earth.

Isaiah 54:4–5

*W*ow! The Lord of Heaven's armies was willing to be a 'husband' to me! Tears of relief flowed knowing that God understood my sorrows and my empty arms and showed me that He would replace human love with His love.

Before they call I will answer; while they are still speaking I will hear.

Isaiah 65:24

This beautiful psalm accompanied many letters to Roy during his illness. They were a great comfort and strength to him at that time.

We live within the shadow of the Almighty,
    sheltered by the God who is above all Gods.

This I declare, that He alone is my refuge, my place of safety; He is my God and I am trusting Him. For He rescues you from every trap, and protects you from the fatal plague. He will shield you with His wings! They will shelter you. His faithful promises are your armour. Now you don't need to be afraid of the dark anymore, nor fear the dangers of the day; nor dread the plagues of darkness, nor disasters in the morning.

Though a thousand fall at my side, though ten thousand are dying around me, the evil will not touch me. I will see how the wicked are punished but I will not share it. For Jehovah is my refuge! I choose the God above all gods to shelter me. How then can evil overtake me or any plague come near? For He orders His angels to protect you wherever you go. They will steady you with their hands to keep you from stumbling against the rocks on the trail. You can safely meet a lion or step on poisonous snakes, yes, even trample them beneath your feet!

For the Lord says, 'Because he loves Me I will rescue him; I will make him great because he trusts in My name. When he calls on Me I

will answer; I will be with him in trouble, and
rescue him and honour him. I will satisfy him
with a full life and give him My salvation.'

Psalm 91

How wonderful it is, how pleasant, when
brothers live in harmony! For harmony is as
precious as the fragrant anointing oil that was
poured over Aaron's head, and ran down onto
his beard, and onto the border of his robe.
Harmony is as refreshing as the dew on Mount
Hermon, on the mountains of Israel. And God
has pronounced this eternal blessing on
Jerusalem, even life for evermore.

Psalm 133

The Rt Rev. David Sheppard, Anglican Bishop of Liverpool and Derek Warlock, Roman Catholic Archbishop of Liverpool, were to me living examples of how to live the Christian life side by side, accepting and learning to understand their differences and at the same time focusing on their unifying points and sharing their deep desire that, through their love, others might come to know the love of Christ for themselves.

Derek Warlock was a Patron of the charity set up in Roy's name for research into lung cancer. Derek himself had been operated on for lung cancer and although the operation was successful and he was able to resume work, he was quite frail. Derek's support and love for Roy was amazing. After Roy died he organised a thanksgiving service at the Liverpool Cathedral, which he affectionately called the Mersey Funnel!

The love and sensitivity with which he prepared and delivered the service was stunning. Anglicans, Catholics and Baptists were represented and the Lord was glorified in it all.

When we read the Gospels, especially Matthew, Mark and Luke, we find the central teaching of Jesus is about the Kingdom of God. He does not immediately say, 'Follow me' when he meets people. By an action or a story he says, 'The Kingdom of God is like this', 'This is my Father's purpose for how the world should be', 'This is what I stand for'. When people have grasped something of his plan, then he says to them, 'Follow me. Join the people of God in the Church who will work together for my Kingdom in the World.'

In Isaiah 58 we are called to be restorers of houses in ruins. This means not just in our church life, but in our family life, so that we can call young people to the adventure of chastity, of faithful, life-long relationships: to restore houses in ruins in our community and public life, so that the needs of the poor and unemployed are not pushed to the margins: to restore houses in ruins in business life, trade unions, in the professions, in education, in law enforcement, so that justice and truth can be relied on: in international affairs so that the poorest countries are given much better resources and trading conditions from countries like ours.

David Sheppard

I am asked to focus on 'discipleship' but in any case I would have settled on that lovely verse about 'a watered garden, like a spring of water, whose waters never fail' (Isaiah 58:11). For me it is special, not so much because of the River Mersey, but because I was brought up in a peaceful Hampshire village where the clear waters of the chalk-streamed River Itchen flowed below, and occasionally watered, our garden. And as a child it fascinated me to think of the source from which each individual droplet of water came to join, as it were, the torrent of grace which moved towards the ocean, keeping our land fertile. You do not have to be a countryman to see what I am getting at: the source of our faith which enlivens and inspires us is our Almighty God himself, infinite, eternal, the Creator, who made us and all about us. And 'discipleship' is all about following the maker's instructions, living them, sharing them.

Let us be clear that the call is not to part-time discipleship: something that we just switch on for a few hours each week, when we have done our work, fulfilled our responsibilities at home, and are free to take up the work of the Gospel as a self-chosen hobby. The call to discipleship is a call to a way of life: at home, at church, at work, in every breath we breathe, in all our relationships, in what we are as well as what we do.

Derek Worlock

Who then can ever keep Christ's love from us? When we have trouble or calamity, when we are hunted down or destroyed, is it because he doesn't love us any more? And if we are hungry, or penniless, or in danger, or threatened with death, has God deserted us?

No, for the Scriptures tell us that for his sake we must be ready to face death at every moment of the day – we are like sheep awaiting slaughter.

But despite all this, overwhelming victory is ours through Christ who loved us enough to die for us. For I am convinced that nothing can ever separate us from his love. Death can't, and life can't. The angels won't, and all the powers of hell itself cannot keep God's love away. Our fears for today, our worries about tomorrow, or where we are – high above the sky, or in the deepest ocean – nothing will ever be able to separate us from the love of God demonstrated by our Lord Jesus Christ when he died for us.

Romans 8:35–39

Roy's favourite Christmas carol was 'In the bleak Midwinter' by Christina Rossetti. The simplicity of it characterised his own life and, poor though he was, he certainly gave his heart ...

In the bleak midwinter
Frosty wind made moan
Earth stood hard as iron,
Water like a stone.
Snow had fallen, snow on snow,
Snow on snow.
In the bleak midwinter
Long ago.

Our God, Heaven cannot hold him
Nor earth sustain.
Heaven and earth shall flee away
When he comes to reign.
In the bleak midwinter
A stable-place sufficed
The Lord God Almighty
Jesus Christ.

Angels and Archangels
May have gathered there,
Cherubim and Seraphim
Thronged the air.
But only His mother
In her maiden bliss
Worshipped the beloved
With a kiss.

What can I give him,
Poor as I am?
If I were a shepherd,
I would bring a lamb.
If I were a wise man,
I would do my part.
Yet what I can I give him –
Give my heart.

Christina Rossetti

The good men perish; the godly die before
their time and no one seems to care or
wonder why. No one seems to realise that
God is taking them away from evil days
ahead. For the godly who die shall rest in
peace.

Isaiah 57:1–2

ABOU BEN ADHEM AND THE ANGEL

Abou Ben Adhem (may his tribe increase!)
Awoke one night from a deep dream of peace,
And saw, within the moonlight in his room,
Making it rich, and like a lily in bloom,
An angel writing in a book of gold:
Exceeding peace had made Ben Adhem bold,
And to the presence in the room he said,
'What writest thou?' – The vision raised its head,
And with a look made of all sweet accord,
Answered, 'The names of those who love the Lord.'
'And is mine one?' said Abou, 'Nay, not so,'
Replied the angel. Abou spoke more low,
But cheerly still; and said, 'I pray thee, then,
Write me as one that loves his fellow-men.'
The angel wrote, and vanished. The next night
It came again with a great wakening light,
And showed the names whom love of God had
    blessed,
And lo! Ben Adhem's name led all the rest.

James Henry Leigh Hunt

This was a poem I loved to recite at school. In the years of our marriage I always felt it applied to Roy. He did love the Lord, but he expressed that love through caring about his fellow man.

I had to refrain from having it read at Roy's funeral because my family had only known of the poem through a Not the Nine O'clock News *sketch and could not have kept a straight face!*

PART TWO

Light

❋ ❋ ❋

O Light that followest all my way,
I yield my flickering torch to thee;
My heart restores its borrowed ray,
That in thy sunshine's blaze its day
May brighter, fairer be.

CROSSING THE BAR

Sunset and evening star,
   And one clear call for me!
And may there be no moaning at the bar,
   When I put out to sea,

But such a tide as moving seems asleep,
   Too full for sound and foam,
When that which drew from out the boundless deep
   Turns again home.

Twilight and evening bell,
   And after that the dark!
And may there be no sadness of farewell
   When I embark;

For tho' from out our bourne of Time and Place
   The flood may bear me far,
I hope to see my Pilot face to face
   When I have crost the bar.

Alfred, Lord Tennyson

THE SHIP

I am standing on the sea shore. A ship at my side spreads her white sails to the morning breeze and starts for the blue ocean. She is an object of beauty and strength, and I stand and watch her till at length she is only a ribbon of white cloud just where the sea and sky come to mingle with each other.

Then someone at my side says, There she is gone! Gone? Gone where? Gone from my sight – that is all – she is just as long in mast and hull and spar as she was when she left my side, and just as able to bear her load of living freight to the place of destination. Her diminished size is in me – not in her, and just at the moment when someone at my side says, 'There! She is gone!' there are other voices ready to take up the glad shout, 'THERE! SHE COMES' –

and that is Dying.

Leonard Lyons

The day thou gavest Lord is ended,
The darkness falls at thy behest.
To thee our morning hymns ascended,
Thy praise shall sanctify our rest.

We thank thee that thy church unsleeping,
While earth rolls onward into light,
Through all the world her watch is keeping
And rests not now by day or night.

As o'er each continent and island
The dawn leads on another day,
The voice of prayer is never silent,
Nor dies the strain of praise away.

The sun that bids us rest is waking
Our brethren 'neath the western sky,
And hour by hour fresh lips are making
Thy wondrous doings heard on high.

So be it Lord; thy throne shall never,
Like earth's proud empires, pass away;
Thy Kingdom stands, and grows forever,
Till all thy creatures own thy sway.

J. Ellerton

O Lord God of our father Israel, praise your name for ever and ever! Yours is the mighty power and glory and victory and majesty. Everything in the heavens and earth is yours, O Lord, and this is your kingdom. We adore you as being in control of everything. Riches and honour come from you alone, and you are the Ruler of all mankind; your hand controls power and might, and it is at your discretion that men are made great and given strength. O our God, we thank you and praise your glorious name.

1 Chronicles 29:10–13

And I said to the man who stood at the gate of the year: 'Give me a light that I may tread safely into the unknown.' And he replied: 'Go out into the darkness and put your hand into the Hand of God. That shall be to you better than light and safer than a known way.' So I went forth and, finding the Hand of God, trod gladly into the night.

Minnie Louise Haskins

'God give them rest in that delightful garden
    where pain
and grief are no more and sighing unknown.'
A prayer that expresses new growth – of life out of
    death
and the refreshment and joy of just being there.
And there are no weeds because it is a heavenly
    garden.

Anon.

*I have included the above because before Roy died he
described a vision he was having, standing in a
most beautiful garden. He said it was indescribable
because it was more beautiful than any garden he
had ever seen on earth. He added, 'I thought I was a
gardener but this gardener's something else!'*

*The following poems I love because they also
remind me of Roy. He was most comfortable in the
countryside and told me endless stories of his
childhood in the Yorkshire moors where the open
landscape provided freedom and, in those days, safety
and security as he and his friends would roam and
play all day.*

*He always felt at peace in his garden. He would
lose all sense of time as he prayed or even worked out
a script or memorised lines, while digging or mowing
or planting.*

GOD OF THE OPEN AIR

These are the things I prize
    And hold of dearest worth:
    Light of the sapphire skies,
    Peace of the silent hills,
Shelter of forests, comfort of the grass,
Music of birds, murmur of little rills,
Shadows of cloud that swiftly pass,
    And, after showers,
    The smell of flowers
    And of the good, brown earth –
And best of all, along the way, friendship and mirth.
    So let me keep
    These treasures of the humble heart
In true possession, owing them by love;
And when at last I can no longer move
    Among them freely, but must part
From the green fields and waters clear,
    Let me not creep
Into some darkened room and hide
From all that makes the world so bright and dear;
    But throw the windows wide
    To welcome in the light;
    And while I clasp a well-belovèd hand,
    Let me once more have sight
    Of the deep sky and the far-smiling land –
    Then gently fall on sleep,
And breathe my body back to Nature's care,
My spirit out to thee, God of the open air.

Henry van Dyke

THE TREE'S PRAYER

Traveller: listen!
I am the wood of your cradle,
the planks of your boat,
the top of your table,
the door of your house,
the handle of your tools,
and the walking stick of your old age.
I am the fruit that nourishes you,
the shade that protects you against the fierce sun,
the refuge of birds that bring joy to your life
and keep your field clear of insects.
I am the beauty of the countryside,
the charm of your garden, the majesty of your
    mountain
the edging of your roads.
I am the firewood that warms you in winter,
the aroma that delights you
and perfumes the air,
I am the health of your body,
the joy of your soul,
and, finally, I am the wood of your coffin.

So, Traveller:
look at me, revel in my beauty,
But don't hurt me.

Translated from the Spanish by Jenny James

Trying to force oneself to be brave will not heal the heart. This is hard for men who are trained to believe that tears are the sign of weakness. But it is forever true that when the storms of life are savage, it is the tree that bends with the wind that survives. Tensing up, walling up the heart, damming up the tears, will inevitably mean trouble later on, perhaps years later. There is emotional release in letting the tears flow.

Catherine Marshall

It is sometimes necessary to have permission to stop grieving; that grieving has been done adequately and life can be picked up again and enjoyed without any feelings of guilt and with a clear conscience. Although this may seem mechanical and even objectionable, a pattern of grief can be formed which becomes a rigid structure and can frustrate any possibility of living freely again.

Jim Graham

Jim Graham was senior Pastor of Gold Hill Baptist Church until 1996 and has been the most incredible friend to our family through thick and thin. I would like to pay tribute to the best bible teacher I have known and for the privilege it has been to sit at his feet and learn.

The Lord is close to those whose hearts are breaking; he rescues those who are humbly sorry for their sins.

The good man does not escape all troubles – he has them too. But the Lord helps him in each and every one.

Psalm 34:18–19

I found this poem when I spent a day in retreat at Highmoor Hall, three months after Roy had died. This book of poems was open at this page in the chapel. It was just what I needed to read that day.

INTO YOUR LIGHT

My outstretched hands are becoming accustomed
to the solitude into which you have thrown me,
more alone
than I could ever bear to be.

I am learning to live
with the death you have chosen for me,
more painful than any death
I have ever chosen to go through.

My eyes are adapting
to the darkness you have chosen for me,
darker than any darkness
I ever knew or chose.

I am learning to recognise
the many disguises of your love,
deeper than any love
I have ever experienced.

And slowly it dawns on me
being lonely is: turning to you
death is: a deep and joyous life
darkness is: finally seeing your light
and love is: being born over and over again.

Ulrich Shaeffer

We are like to Him with whom there is no past or future, with whom a day is as a thousand years, and a thousand years as one day, when we do our work in the great present, leaving both past and future to Him to whom they are ever present, and fearing nothing, because He is in our future as much as He is in our past, as much as, and far more than, we can feel Him to be in our present. Partakers thus of the divine nature, resting in that perfect All-in-all in whom our nature is eternal too, we walk without fear, full of hope and courage and strength to do His will, waiting for the endless good which He is always giving as fast as He can get us able to take it in.

George MacDonald

*A*s Roy grew weaker and his death more imminent, I began to wonder whether people's prayers for his healing were appropriate. Was this the way God wanted it? As I asked God about it, I sensed Him saying 'What are days? What are years?' I suddenly saw the timelessness of God in a new way. I realised that the day Roy died, whether it was in a week or ten years, would be the day God decided Roy's life on earth was complete. It was in His hands and I could rest my case.

TREASURES OF DARKNESS

Within the depths of
His darkest clouds
God often seems to bury His
richest treasures –
    silver streaks of growth,
    sterling faith,
    precious gleaming truths –
for his beloved children.
Has a dense cloud of
    doubt,
    pain,
    loss,
    trouble,
    frustration or
    loneliness
Settled over you, dear one?
Search out the treasures of darkness!
The riches of your Heavenly Father, hide there
With your name engraved in silver!

Susan Lenzkes

And I will give you treasures hidden in the darkness, secret riches; and you will know that I am doing this – I, the Lord, the God of Israel, the one who calls you by your name.

Isaiah 45:3

Faith must be tested, because it can be turned into a personal possession only through conflict. What is your faith up against just now? The test will either prove that your faith is right, or it will kill it. 'Blessed is he whosoever shall not be offended in Me.' The final thing is confidence in Jesus. Believe steadfastly on Him and all you come up against will develop your faith. There is continual testing in the life of faith, and the last great test is death. May God keep us in fighting trim! Faith is unutterable trust in God which never dreams that He will not stand by us.

Oswald Chambers

The next two passages were found in a little old-fashioned book called Daily Strength for Daily Needs *by Mary W. Tileston, which has been a blessing to me.*

We have very little command over the circumstances in which we may be called by God to bear our part – unlimited command over the temper of our souls, but next to no command over the outward forms of trial. The most energetic will cannot order the events by which our spirits are to be perilled and tested. Powers quite beyond our reach – death, accident, fortune, another's sin – may change in a moment all the conditions of our life. With tomorrow's sun existence may have new and awful aspects for any of us.

J. H. Thom

It is not by seeking more fertile regions where toil is lighter – happier circumstances free from difficult complications and troublesome people – but by bringing the high courage of a devout soul, clear in principle and aim, to bear upon what is given to us, that we brighten our inward light, lead something of a true life, and introduce the kingdom of heaven into the midst of our earthly day. If we cannot work out the will of God where God has placed us, then why has he placed us there?

J. H. Thom

THE ROAD NOT TAKEN

Two roads diverged in a yellow wood,
And sorry I could not travel both
And be one traveller, long I stood
And looked down as far as I could
To where it bent in the undergrowth;

Then took the other, as just as fair,
And having perhaps the better claim,
Because it was grassy and wanted wear:
Though as for that the passing there
Had worn them really about the same,

And both that morning equally lay
In leaves no step had trodden black.
Oh, I kept the first for another day!
Yet knowing how way leads on to way,
I doubted if I should ever come back.

I shall be telling this with a sigh
Somewhere ages and ages hence:
Two roads diverged in a wood, and I –
I took the one less travelled by,
And that has made all the difference.

Robert Frost

Since the Lord is directing our steps, why try
to understand everything that happens along
the way?

Proverbs 20:24

You are laying up treasure in heaven or upon
earth. Everything you have you must
ultimately lose. Everything you invest in the
souls of men, you will save. You are going to
enter heaven either a pauper, having sent
nothing ahead, or as one who is to receive an
inheritance, made possible by contributions
laid up while still upon earth.

Oswald J. Smith

He is no fool who gives what he cannot keep
in order to gain what he cannot lose.

Jim Elliot

*(Jim Elliot and his companions were speared to death
by Auca Indians in Equador.)*

Never consider whether you are of use – but
ever consider you are not your own but His.

Oswald Chambers

The following words, written to me in a letter by a dear missionary friend when I was a young Christian, are now indelibly imprinted in my memory.

Referring to taking photographs, what we *focus on* looms largest and other things fade into the periphery. Likewise in spiritual matters. *Whatever* we focus on is magnified, whether it's our faults and failings or our problems – or the faults and failings of others. That's why Paul exhorts us to keep our eyes firmly focused on Jesus, so that *He* is magnified and other things fade into perspective.

Key thought: whatever gets your attention, gets you!

I play so many games,
I have so many faces,
I run so many races
That need not be run by me ...

I talk so many ways,
I know so many stories,
I sing so many ballads
That need not be sung by me ...

Oh Lord, dear Lord, great author of the play,
May I in wisdom learn the only part that I need play
Is the part that you wrote for me
Is the part that you wrote for me.

You've given me the lives,
You've shown the right direction,
You gave me a reflection
Of what I need to say.

So many want to lead
And so many times I follow.
Lord let me not be hollow
Like men in those other plays.

Oh Lord, dear Lord, great author of the play,
May I in wisdom learn the only part that I need play
Is the part that you wrote for me
Is the part that you wrote for me.

Joni Eareckson

*H*aving had a show business background, I love
this song which Joni sang on her album, Joni. Roy
had a similar parable, that God is the composer, Jesus

the conductor and we are all the players of music.
Some of us are called to play solos, some noisy, some
quiet, some will be percussion and make only one
small contribution to the piece, but if each musician
plays to the best of his ability the part written for him
the whole symphony will sound wonderful – just the
way the composer intended it to sound, but we need
to keep our eyes on the conductor all the time.

Be patterns, be examples in all countries,
places, islands, nations, wherever you come,
that your carriage and life may preach among
all sorts of people and to them; then you will
come to walk cheerfully over the world,
answering that of God in every one.

George Fox

That was sent to me by a dear friend as I embarked
on a world tour in aid of the Roy Castle Lung
Cancer Foundation. She knew my apprehension as I
contemplated such a task and these words from the
seventeenth century gave me more reassurance than
she ever could have realised.

It reminded me of words my mother had used
many times through my growing years, that wherever
I went I was to be an example for good and that
abroad I was an ambassador for Great Britain! When
I became a Christian I was aware of the awesome
responsibility we have knowing 'we are Christ's
Ambassadors' (2 Corinthians 5:20).

This is a passage from another book by Oswald Chambers. He was a well respected bible teacher and, although he died in 1917, his spiritual insight continues to be relevant today.

The awful problem of suffering continually crops up in the Scriptures, and in life and remains a mystery. From Job until now, and from before Job, the mystery of suffering remains. And always, after the noisy clamour of the novice in suffering, and after the words of weight of the veteran; after the sarcasm and cynicism and bitterness of more or less pained people, aye, and after the slander of Satan against God – the voice of the Spirit sounds clear, 'Have you considered My servant Job?'

Perhaps to be able to explain suffering is the clearest indication of never having suffered. Sin, suffering, and sanctification are not problems of the mind, but facts of life – mysteries that awaken all other mysteries until the heart rests in God, and waiting patiently knows 'He does all things well.' Oh, the unspeakable joy of knowing that God reigns! that He is our Father, and that the clouds are but 'the dust of His feet'! Religious life is based and built up and matured on primal implicit trust, transfigured by Love; the explicit statement of that life can only be made by the spectator, never by the saint.

Oswald Chambers

Then the Lord answered Job ... 'Where
were you when I laid the foundations of the
earth? Tell me if you know so much. Do you
know how its dimensions were determined,
and who did the surveying? What supports
its foundations, and who laid its cornerstone,
as the morning stars sang together and all
the angels shouted for joy?'

Job 38:4–7

(And read on ...!)

My Utmost for His Highest *is a compilation of
teachings by Oswald Chambers, arranged into a
thought for each day of the year for daily devotions. I
became a Christian in 1975 and I suppose I have read
it most days since then. I am amazed that it still
comes with a freshness and appropriateness for each
day.*

*Here is one passage which I have found very
helpful in dealing with sorrows and suffering.*

RECEIVING ONE'S SELF IN THE
FIRES OF SORROW

What shall I say? Father, save me from this
hour? But for this cause came I unto this
hour. Father, glorify Thy name.

John 12:27–28

My attitude as a saint to sorrow and difficulty is not to ask that they may be prevented, but to ask that I may preserve the self God created me to be through every fire of sorrow. Our Lord received Himself in the fire of sorrow, He was saved not *from* the hour, but *out* of the hour.

We say that there ought to be no sorrow, but there *is* sorrow, and we have to receive ourselves in its fires. If we try and evade sorrow, refuse to lay our account with it, we are foolish. Sorrow is one of the biggest facts in life; it is no use saying sorrow ought not to be. Sin and sorrow and suffering *are*, and it is not for us to say that God has made a mistake in allowing them.

Sorrow burns up a great amount of shallowness, but it does not always make a man better. Suffering either gives me my self or it destroys my self. You cannot receive your self in success, you lose your head; you cannot receive your self in monotony, you grouse. The way to find your self is in the fires of sorrow. Why it should be so is another matter, but that it is so is true in the Scriptures and in human experience. You always know the man who has been through the fires of sorrow and received himself, you are certain you can go to him in trouble and find that he has ample leisure for you. If a man has not been through the fires of sorrow, he is apt to be contemptuous, he has no time for you. If you receive yourself in

the fires of sorrow, God will make you
nourishment for other people.

Oswald Chambers

Our deepest fear is not that we are inadequate.
Our deepest fear is that we are powerful beyond
measure. It is our light, not our darkness, that
most frightens us. We ask ourselves who am I to
be brilliant, gorgeous, talented and fabulous?
Actually who are you *not* to be?

You are a child of God. Your playing small
does not serve the world. There's nothing
enlightened about shrinking so that other
people won't feel secure around you. We were
born to make manifest the glory of God that is
within us. It's not just in some of us; it's in
everyone. And as we let our light shine we
unconsciously give light to other people to do
the same. As we are liberated from our fear our
presence automatically liberates others.

Nelson Mandela

*That was from Nelson Mandela's inaugural speech. I
had the privilege of meeting Nelson Mandela
recently when I visited Cape Town. The words above
his coat of arms outside his residence read 'The Reward
of Valour'. It moved me to tears when I considered the
years he endured in prison, holding onto and believing
in his dream of a different South Africa and now he is
reaping the reward of all that suffering.*

Matthew 11:28–29 Are you tired? Worn out? Burned out on religion? Come to me. Get away with me and you'll recover your life. I'll show you how to take a real rest. Walk with me and work with me and watch how I do it. Learn the unforced rhythms of grace. I won't lay anything heavy or ill-fitting on you. Keep company with me and you'll learn to live freely and lightly.

Eugene Peterson

They that wait upon the Lord shall renew their strength. They shall mount up with wings as eagles; they shall run and not be weary, they shall walk and not faint.

Isaiah 40:31

DEATH

Death be not proud, though some have called thee
Mighty and dreadful, for thou art not so;
For those whom thou think'st thou dost overthrow
Die not, poor Death; nor yet canst thou kill me.
From Rest and Sleep, which but thy pictures be,
Much pleasure, then from thee much more must
    flow;
And soonest our best men with thee do go –
Rest of their bones and soul's delivery!
Thou'rt slave to fate, chance, kings and desperate
    men
And dost with poison, war, and sickness dwell;
And poppy or charms can make us sleep as well
And better than thy stroke. Why swell'st thou then?
One short sleep past, we wake eternally,
And death shall be no more: Death, thou shalt die!

John Donne

It'll be easier when …
The baby is born
He sleeps through the night
His teeth are all through
And he understands 'no',
It'll be easier then.

It'll be easier when …
He's started to walk
He's dry through the night
He's got over the mumps
He goes off to school.
It'll be easier then.

It'll be easier when …
He's passed his exams
He's into his teens
He's got over the humps
He drives his own car.
It'll be easier then.

It'll be easier when …
He's gone off to college
Got his own flat
The house is our own
We're a couple again.
It'll be easier then.

It'll be easier when …
The old man's retired
The children are married
The pressure is off
We've more leisure time.
It'll be easier then …

Is it easier now
that the playroom stands empty
The music is soft
The bedrooms are tidy
There's room in the loft?
Yes it's easier now.

Is it easier now
As I sit back and wonder
What I did with my day
Things that seemed more important
Than stories and play.
It's both foolish and tragic
To wish time away.
Oh yes ...
It's much easier now.

I wrote these words because we all think that once we've got over the present hurdle, life will become easier, less pressured and we'll be more able to cope. But the reality is that as soon as we have jumped one hurdle we have to build up the energy and resources to face and jump the next one. A wise friend said to me one day that many people live their lives as if they are doing a dress rehearsal, whereas today is the real thing. We can't go back and improve on it, we can only regret we didn't perform very well.

You might as well be useful where you are, because you certainly can be of no use where you are not.

Oswald Chambers

Look here, you people who say, 'Today or tomorrow we are going to such and such a town, stay there a year and open up a profitable business.' How do you know what is going to happen tomorrow? For the length of your lives is as uncertain as the morning mist – now you see it; soon it is gone. What you ought to say is 'If the Lord wants us to, we shall live and do this or that.' Otherwise you will be bragging about your own plans and such self-confidence never pleases God.

James 4:13–16

We can make our plans, but the final outcome is in God's hands.

Proverbs 16:1

PART THREE

Joy

✳ ✳ ✳

O Joy that seekest me through pain,
I cannot close my heart to thee;
I trace the rainbow through the rain,
And feel the promise is not vain
That morn shall tearless be.

Joy is peace dancing.
Peace is joy resting.

Jim Graham

*Abide in Me, and I in you. As the branch
cannot bear fruit of itself, unless it abides in
the vine, neither can you, unless you abide in
Me ... These things I have spoken to you, that
My joy may remain in you, and that your joy
may be full.*

John 15:4,11

Christ Himself is the source of joy. The sap
of the vine that surges into the branches is
grace-unqualified love. The words *grace* and
joy come from the same Greek root. Joy is
the delight of being loved. Everything that
Christ said and did and continues to do in
our lives today tells us that we are cherished,
valued, and loved. He died for us, rose from
the dead for us, and is with us now and is
ready to heal us with accepting and affirming
love.

There is no authentic joy apart from
being loved by Christ. His joy persists
regardless of life's circumstances. On the
other hand, happiness is conditioned by
what's happening to and around us. The
word *happiness* comes from *hap* ('chance'),
and chances change. That's why there is such
a great difference between happiness and joy.
Life is undependable; human affection is
often conditioned by our adequacy or
performance, and situations we counted on
remaining stable can fluctuate and scuttle
our carefully laid plans.

Whenever our security is in people or possessions, we may know a measure of happiness for a time, but not joy. That precious spiritual gift is the result of experiencing a love that will never change, that not even our failures will diminish in the least degree and that will remain constant whatever people do or say to hurt us. Where do you find a love like that? Only in Christ. And from that gracious love joy flows.

Lloyd Ogilvie

Pure joy comes only from the heartbreak of Calvary.

This is too glorious, too wonderful to believe! I can NEVER be lost to your Spirit! I can NEVER get away from my God! If I go up to heaven, you are there; if I go down to the place of the dead, you are there. If I ride the morning winds to the farthest oceans, even there your hand will guide me, your strength will support me. If I try to hide in the darkness, the night becomes light around me. For even the darkness cannot hide from God; to you the night shines as bright as day. Darkness and light are both alike to you.

Psalm 139:6–12

The Psalm-writer sounds so excited as he makes these discoveries! How wonderful to know we have a God who is always *present and knows in detail everything that is happening in our lives.*

SAFETY

Dear! of all happy in the hour, most blest
    He who has found our hid security,
Assured in the dark tides of the world that rest,
    And heard our word, 'Who is so safe as we?'
We have found safety with all things undying,
    The winds, and morning, tears of men and mirth,
The deep night, and birds singing, and clouds flying,
    And sleep, and freedom, and the autumnal earth.

We have built a house that is not for Time's
      throwing.
    We have gained a peace unshaken by pain for ever.
War knows no power. Safe shall be my going,
    Secretly armed against all death's endeavour;
Safe though all safety's lost; safe where men fall;
And if these poor limbs die, safest of all.

Rupert Brooke

If I should go before the rest of you,
Break not a flower nor inscribe a stone,
Nor when I'm gone speak in a Sunday voice,
But be the usual selves that I have known.
Weep if you must,
Parting is hell,
But life goes on,
So sing as well.

Joyce Grenfell

I believe in the sun even when it is not shining
I believe in love even when I feel it not.
I believe in God even when He is silent.

Words found written on a cellar wall
in Cologne after World War II

FOR THE FALLEN.

With proud thanksgiving, a mother for her children,
    England mourns for her dead across the sea.
Flesh of her flesh they were, spirit of her spirit,
    Fallen in the cause of the free.

Solemn the drums thrill: Death august and royal
    Sings sorrow up into immortal spheres.
There is music in the midst of desolation
    And a glory that shines upon our tears.

They went with songs to the battle, they were young,
    Straight of limb, true of eye, steady and aglow.
They were staunch to the end against odds
    uncounted,
    They fell with their faces to the foe.

They shall grow not old, as we that are left grow old:
    Age shall not weary them, nor the years condemn.
At the going down of the sun and in the morning
    We will remember them.

They mingle not with their laughing comrades again;
    They sit no more at familiar tables of home;
They have no lot in our labour of the day-time:
    They sleep beyond England's foam.

But where our desires are and our hopes profound,
    Felt as a well-spring that is hidden from sight,
To the innermost heart of their own land they are
    known
    As the stars are known to the Night;

As the stars that shall be bright when we are dust,
  Moving in marches upon the heavenly plain,
As the stars that are starry in the time of our
  darkness,
  To the end, to the end, they remain.

Laurence Binyon

Having been born at the beginning of the war, I have wept many a time on Armistice Day as the Fallen are remembered – son separated from mother, husband from wife, father from young family – the pain, the loss, the ache, the sacrifice become very vivid.

My mother, as a doctor's wife in a small town, spent many an hour consoling the bereaved in their homes. I, as a small child, was left outside on the doorstep to wonder …

The fourth verse has become very personal to me as I often recite it with gratitude in my heart to God that Roy has been spared the indignities of old age and died while he still had much to contribute to life. What a way to go!

Always give thanks for everything to our God and Father in the name of our Lord Jesus Christ.

Ephesians 5:20.

There is a right time for everything;
A time to be born;
A time to die;
A time to plant;
A time to harvest;
A time to kill;
A time to heal;
A time to destroy;
A time to rebuild;
A time to cry;
A time to laugh;
A time to grieve;
A time to dance;
A time for scattering stones;
A time for gathering stones;
A time to hug;
A time not to hug;
A time to find;
A time to lose;
A time for keeping;
A time for throwing away;
A time to tear;
A time to repair;
A time to be quiet;
A time to speak up;
A time for loving;
A time for hating;
A time for war;
A time for peace.

What does one really get from hard work? I
have thought about this in connection with
all the various kinds of work God has given
to mankind. Everything is appropriate in its

own time. But though God has planted eternity in the hearts of men, even so, man cannot see the whole scope of God's work from beginning to end.

Ecclesiastes 3:1–11

Isn't it strange that princes and kings,
And clowns that caper in sawdust rings,
And ordinary folk like you and me
Are builders for eternity.
And each is given a bag of tools;
An hour-glass and a book of rules.
And each must build e'er his time has flown
A stumbling-block or a stepping-stone

All the world's a stage,
And all the men and women merely players:
They have their exits and their entrances;
And one man in his time plays many parts,
His acts being seven ages. At first the infant,
Mewling and puking in the nurse's arms.
Then the whining school-boy, with his satchel,
And shining morning face, creeping like snail
Unwillingly to school. And then the lover,
Sighing like furnace, with a woeful ballad
Made to his mistress' eyebrow. Then a soldier,
Full of strange oaths, and bearded like the pard,
Jealous in honour, sudden and quick in quarrel,

Seeking the bubble reputation
Even in the cannon's mouth. And then the justice,
In fair round belly with good capon lined,
With eyes severe, and beard of formal cut,
Full of wise saws and modern instances;
And so he plays his part. The sixth age shifts
Into the lean and slipper'd pantaloon,
With spectacles on nose and pouch on side,
His youthful hose, well saved, a world too wide
For his shrunk shank; and his big manly voice,
Turning again toward childish treble, pipes
And whistles in his sound. Last scene of all,
That ends this strange eventful history,
Is second childishness and mere oblivion,
Sans teeth, sans eyes, sans taste, sans every thing.

William Shakespeare

I studied As You Like It for my O Levels many years ago. I was always fascinated by Jaques' seven ages of man speech. It is so up to date and observant, it could almost have been written this century. It also made me realise that, although technology and medical science might advance, life in all its stages changes not at all – including the fact that poems learnt in childhood stay with you forever, while something learnt yesterday has disappeared today!

Don't be anxious about tomorrow. God will take care of your tomorrow too. Live one day at a time.

Matthew 6:34.

Oh, ask not thou, How shall I bear
The burden of to-morrow?
Sufficient for to-day, its care,
Its evil and its sorrow;
God imparteth by the way
Strength sufficient for the day.

J. E. Saxby

What happiness for those whose guilt has been forgiven! What joys when sins are covered over! What relief for those who have confessed their sins and God has cleared their record.

There was a time when I wouldn't admit what a sinner I was. But my dishonesty made me miserable and filled my days with frustration. All day and all night your hand was heavy on me. My strength evaporated like water on a sunny day, until I finally admitted all my sins to you and stopped trying to hide them. I said to myself, 'I will confess them to the Lord.' And you forgave me! All my guilt is gone.

Now I say that each believer should confess his sins to God when he is aware of them while there is time to be forgiven. Judgment will not touch him if he does.

You are my hiding place from every storm of life; you even keep me from getting into trouble. You surround me with songs of victory. I will instruct you (says the Lord) and guide you along the best pathway for your life; I will advise you and watch your progress. Don't be like a senseless horse or mule that has to have a bit in its mouth to keep it in line!

Many sorrows come to the wicked, but abiding love surrounds those who trust in the Lord. So rejoice in him all those who are his, and shout for joy all those who try to obey him.

Psalm 32

Snow in January
Looking for ledges
To hide in unmelted.

February evening:
A cold puddle of petrol
Makes its own rainbow.

Wind in March:
No leaves left
For its stiff summons.

April sunlight:
Even the livid bricks
Muted a little.

Wasp in May
Storing his venom
For a long summer.

Morning in June:
On the sea's horizon
A white island, alone.

July evening:
Sour reek of beer
Warm by the river.

August morning:
A squirrel leaps and
Only one branch moves.

September chestnuts:
Falling too early,
Split white before birth.

October garden:
At the top of the tree
A thrush stabs an apple.

November morning:
A whiff of cordite
Caught in the leaf mould.

Sun in December:
In his box of straw
The tortoise wakes.

Anthony Thwaite

We know how happy they are now because they stayed true to him then, even though they suffered greatly for it. Job is an example of a man who continued to trust the Lord in sorrow; from his experiences we can see how the Lord's plan finally ended in good, for he is full of tenderness and mercy.

James 5:11

*T*his beautiful hymn was one Roy and I chose for our wedding. I remember the organist at a rehearsal laughing cynically and saying he couldn't understand why so many couples came to the altar and asked God to 'forgive their foolish ways'. Well, read on dear organist. I believe that unless we are following the Lord, all our ways must seem foolishness to Him. But once we have a relationship with Him, He enables us to let go of the strain and stress so that our lives may confess the beauty of His peace.

Dear Lord and Father of Mankind,
Forgive our foolish ways!
Re-clothe us in our rightful mind.
In purer lives thy service find,
In deeper reverence praise.

In simple trust like theirs who heard
Beside the Syrian Sea
The gracious calling of the Lord,
Let us, like them, without a word
Rise up and follow thee.

O Sabbath rest by Galilee!
O calm of hills above,
Where Jesus knelt to share with thee
The silence of eternity,
Interpreted by love.

Drop thy still dews of quietness
Till all our strivings cease;
Take from our souls the strain and stress
And let our ordered lives confess
The beauty of thy peace.

Breathe through the heats of our desire
Thy coolness and thy balm
Let sense be dumb, let flesh retire
Speak through the earthquake, wind and fire
O still small voice of calm!

J. G. Whittier

Thou wilt keep him in perfect peace whose
mind is stayed on thee.

Isaiah 26:3.

This was my favourite song to sing, very early in the morning on the beach at Bournemouth! It was one of the few times I would have the beach to myself, apart from the occasional dog-walker or student sweeping sand off the promenade.

I decided that you can't say the word Jesus over and over and remain miserable! As I sang the words I realised how very sweet Jesus' name is and that it really does all the things the hymn suggests once we believe in Him.

How sweet the name of Jesus sounds
In a believer's ear
It soothes his sorrows, heals his wounds
And drives away his fear.

It makes the wounded spirit whole
And calms the troubled breast,
Tis manna to the hungry soul
And to the weary – rest.

Dear name, the Rock on which I build
My shield and hiding place,
My never failing treasury filled
With boundless stores of grace.

Jesus my Shepherd, Husband, Friend,
My Prophet, Priest and King,
My Lord, my Life, my Way, my End,
Accept the praise I bring.

Weak is the effort of my heart
And cold my warmest thought;
But when I see thee as thou art,
I'll praise thee as I ought.

Till then I would Thy love proclaim
With every fleeting breath
And may the music of thy name
Refresh my soul in death.

J. Newton

He turned my mourning
into dancing again,
He's lifted my sorrows,
I can't stay silent.
I must sing for His joy has come.

Where there once was only hurt
He gave His healing hand,
Where there once was only pain
He brought comfort like a friend.
I feel the sweetness of His love
Piercing my darkness.
I see the bright and morning sun
As it ushers in His joyful gladness. (*twice*)

Your anger lasts for a moment in time
But your favour is here
And will be on me for all my lifetime. (*twice*)

Tommy Walker

*R*oy and I first heard this wonderful song when we
had the privilege of speaking at some meetings
with the Evangelist Luis Palau. As we entered the
church a huge choir was singing this song and the
whole place was rocking to the music – Roy and I
were filled with such joy we almost danced up the
aisle!

I knew, when we were planning his thanksgiving
service that we had to include it – so that people's
mourning could be turned into dancing. It caused
some surprise and a few raised eyebrows but soon
everyone was enjoying the joyful mood as the song

was lovingly sung by a member of Remission Gospel Choir, Carl McGregor. Thank you Lord for lifting our sorrows.

Then he turned my sorrow into joy! He took away my clothes of mourning and gave me gay and festive garments to rejoice in so that I might sing glad praises to the Lord instead of lying in silence in the grave. O Lord my God, I will keep thanking you forever.

Psalm 30:11–12

Our hearts ache, but at the same time we have the joy of the Lord. We are poor, but we give rich spiritual gifts to others. We own nothing, and yet we enjoy everything.

We confidently and joyfully look forward actually to becoming all that God has had in mind for us to be. We ... rejoice, too, when we run into problems and trials.

Trust him; and even now you are happy with the inexpressible joy that comes from heaven itself.

Though they have been going through much trouble and hard times, they have mixed their wonderful joy with their deep poverty, and the result has been an overflow of giving to others.

Though I did nothing to deserve it, and though I am the most useless Christian there is, yet I was the one chosen for this special joy of telling the Gentiles the Glad News of the endless treasures available to them in Christ.

God has chosen poor people to be rich in faith, and the kingdom of heaven is theirs, for that is the gift God has promised to all those who love him.

God is able to make it up to you by giving you everything you need and more, so that there will not only be enough for your own needs, but plenty left over to give joyfully to others.

2 Cor 6:10; Rom 5:2,3; 1Pet 1:8; 2 Cor 8:2; Eph 3:8; Jas 2:5; 2 Cor 9:8 (taken from Living Lights*)*

I'VE GOT FRIENDS IN HIGH PLACES

I've got hope when things look bad
And I can smile when I should be sad,
I've got friends who lift me up when I'm feeling low
And they watch over me wherever I may go.

I've got friends in High Places,
So high, but not so far away.
I've got friends in High Places
And I'm gonna be with them some day.

There's the Father right by His Son
And the Angels, each and every one,
And other friends I miss so much and long to see,
But knowing I'll be with them one day comforts me.

I've got friends in High Places ...

Why should I run?
Why should I hide?
What's there to fear
When my friends are on my side?

I've got friends in High Places ...

Archie Jordan and Austin Roberts

When we know we have that certain hope of Eternal Life Jesus has promised us, we don't need to be afraid of the separation death brings.

I love to sing this song (in my car with the windows wound up) along with Larnelle Harris, who *is my favourite Gospel singer, and rejoice that Roy is now in High Places, seated with Christ!*

I pray that you will begin to understand how incredibly great his power is to help those who believe him. It is that same mighty power that raised Christ from the dead and seated him in the place of honour at God's right hand in heaven, far, far above any other king or ruler or dictator or leader. Yes, his honour is far more glorious than that of anyone else either in this world or in the world to come.

Ephesians 1:19–21

And [God] lifted us up from the grave into glory along with Christ, where we sit with him in the heavenly realms – all because of what Christ Jesus did.

Ephesians 2:6.

O let the Son of God enfold you
With His Spirit and His love.
Let Him fill your heart and satisfy your soul.
O let Him have the things that hold you,
And His Spirit like a dove
Will descend upon your life and make you whole.

Jesus, O Jesus, Come and fill your lambs.
Jesus, O Jesus, Come and fill your lambs.

O come and sing this song with gladness
As your hearts are filled with joy,
Lift your hands in sweet surrender to His name.
O give Him all your tears and sadness,
Give Him all your years of pain,
And you'll enter into life in Jesus' name.

Jesus, O Jesus, Come and fill your lambs.
Jesus, O Jesus, Come and fill your lambs.

John Wimber

I still find it difficult to sing this beautiful song
*without crying. I am grateful for songs which evoke
tears, releasing emotions into the loving arms of the
Saviour.*

*I am also grateful to John Wimber of the Vineyard
Fellowship in California for the example of his
courage as he faced his own battle with cancer.*

May your strength match the length of your days.

Deuteronomy 33:25

He that hath so many causes of joy, and so great, is very much in love with sorrow and peevishness, who loses all these pleasures, and chooses to sit down upon his little handful of thorns. Enjoy the blessings of this day, if God sends them; and the evils of it bear patiently and sweetly: for this day is only ours, we are dead to yesterday, and we are not yet born to the morrow. But if we look abroad, and bring into one day's thoughts the evil of many, certain and uncertain, what will be and what will never be, our load will be as intolerable as it is unreasonable.

Jeremy Taylor

When peace like a river attendeth my way,
When sorrows like sea-billows roll;
Whatever my lot you have taught me to say,
'It is well, it is well with my soul.'

Though Satan should buffet, if trials should come,
Let this blessed assurance control,
That Christ has regarded my helpless estate,
And has shed his own blood for my soul.

My sin – O the bliss of this glorious thought –
My sin – not in part – but the whole
Is nailed to his cross; and I bear it no more;
Praise the Lord, praise the Lord, O my soul.

For me, be it Christ, be it Christ hence to live!
If Jordan above me shall roll,
No pang shall be mine, for in death as in life
You will whisper your peace to my soul.

But Lord, it's for you – for your coming we wait,
The sky, not the grave, is our goal:
O trump of the angel! O voice of the Lord!
Blessed hope! blessed rest of my soul.

Horatio Spafford

*H*oratio Spafford wrote this at a time of great
personal tragedy. It was inspiring to hear it sung by
Joni Eareckson who, in spite of being paralysed from the
neck down, is gifted with her voice, with her ability to
paint by mouth, as well as her talent as a writer. God
has used her infirmity to bless others and to glorify Him.

The antithesis of boredom is joy.
It is constant regardless of where we are
or what we have.
Joy is unassailable, undiminishable
by circumstances.
It's the special gift of union with
Christ, the Life.
With His joy we can face difficulties,
deal with impossible situations,
and endure the most drab,
uninspiring, mundane
circumstances of life.
Joy is the identifiable outward sign of
the inner experience of grace.
A joyless Christian is a
contradiction of terms!

Lloyd Ogilvie

The writings of Lloyd Ogilvie have blessed me on a daily basis for some years, especially Turning your Struggles into Stepping Stones. *He is now Chaplain to the Senate in Washington DC.*

SONG

When I am dead, my dearest,
Sing no sad songs for me;
Plant thou no roses at my head,
Nor shady cypress tree:
Be the green grass above me
With showers and dewdrops wet;

And if thou wilt, remember,
   And if thou wilt, forget.

I shall not see the shadows,
   I shall not fear the rain;
I shall not hear the nightingale
   Sing on as if in pain;
And dreaming through the twilight
   That doth not rise nor set,
Haply I may remember,
   And haply may forget.

Christina Rossetti

REMEMBER

Remember me when I am gone away,
   Gone far away into the silent land;
   When you can no more hold me by the hand,
Nor I half turn to go yet turning stay.
Remember me when no more day by day
   You tell me of our future that you planned:
   Only remember me; you understand
It will be late to counsel then or pray.
Yet if you should forget me for a while
   And afterwards remember, do not grieve:
   For if the darkness and corruption leave
   A vestige of the thoughts that once I had,
Better by far you should forget and smile
   Than that you should remember and be sad.

Christina Rossetti

When you walk through the storm
Hold your head up high
And don't be afraid of the dark.
At the end of the storm
Is a golden sky
And the sweet silver song of a lark.
Walk on through the wind
Walk on through the rain
Though your dreams be tossed and blown.
Walk on, walk on with hope in your heart
And you'll never walk alone
You'll never walk alone.

Oscar Hammerstein

When I first saw the film Carousel I was glad to have gone alone as I bawled my eyes out all the way through! Surely Oscar Hammerstein must be one of the greatest lyricists this century.

Whether this song is sung by Liverpool supporters out of sentiment, or because it has become synonymous with the game, the words never fail to move me and to remind me that I am never alone.

So I pray for you Gentiles that God who gives you hope will keep you happy and full of peace as you believe in him. I pray that God will help you overflow with hope in him through the Holy Spirit's power within you.

Romans 15:13

104

DAFFODILS

I wandered lonely as a cloud
　　That floats on high o'er vales and hills,
When all at once I saw a crowd,
　　A host, of golden daffodils;
Beside the lake, beneath the trees,
Fluttering and dancing in the breeze.

Continuous as the stars that shine
　　And twinkle on the Milky Way,
They stretched in never-ending line
　　Along the margin of a bay:
Ten thousand saw I at a glance,
Tossing their heads in sprightly dance.

The waves beside them danced, but they
　　Out-did the sparkling waves in glee:
A poet could not but be gay,
　　In such a jocund company:
I gazed – and gazed – but little thought
What wealth the show to me had brought:

For oft, when on my couch I lie
　　In vacant or in pensive mood,
They flash upon that inward eye
　　Which is the bliss of solitude;
And then my heart with pleasure fills,
And dances with the daffodils.

William Wordsworth

I *included the above poem because for me it's like breathing in big gulps of beautiful fresh country air. I suppose it is Wordsworth's most famous poem and for good reason. Anyone who has spent time walking in the Lake District knows the pure joy that walking amongst such wild and awesome scenery can bring.*

But all shall be well, and all shall be well and all manner of things shall be well.

Dame Julian of Norwich

YE ARE NOT YOUR OWN?

Know thee not ... ye are not your own?

1 Cor 6:19

There is no such thing as a private life – 'a world within the world' – for a man or woman who is brought into fellowship with Jesus Christ's sufferings. God breaks up the private life of His saints, and makes it a thoroughfare for the world on the one hand and for Himself on the other. No human being can stand that unless he is identified with Jesus Christ. We are not sanctified for ourselves, we are called into the fellowship of the Gospel, and things happen which have nothing to do with us, God is getting us into fellowship with Himself. Let Him have his way, if you do not, instead of being of the slightest use to God in His

Redemptive work in the world, you will be a hindrance and a clog.

The first thing God does with us is to get us based on rugged Reality until we do not care what becomes of us individually as long as He gets His way for the purpose of His Redemption. Why shouldn't we go through heartbreaks? Through these doorways God is opening up ways of fellowship with His Son. Most of us fall and collapse at the first grip of pain; we sit down on the threshold of God's purpose and die away of self-pity, and all so-called Christian sympathy will aid us to our death-bed. But God will not. He comes with the grip of the pierced hand of His Son, and says – 'Enter into fellowship with Me; arise and shine.' If through a broken heart God can bring His purposes to pass in the world, then thank Him for breaking your heart.

Oswald Chambers

Always give thanks for everything to our God and Father in the name of our Lord Jesus Christ.

Ephesians 5:20.

I learned this lesson many years ago when I first read this. It taught me that we should never stay silent, if by sharing our own lives with others, we can point them to Jesus Christ.

A SHEPHERD LOOKS AT
THE 23RD PSALM

Yea though I walk through the valley of the shadow of death I will fear no evil for thou art with me.

As Christians we will sooner or later discover that it is in the valleys of our lives that we find refreshment from God Himself. It is not until we have walked with Him through some very deep troubles that we discover He can lead us to find our refreshment in Him right there in the midst of our difficulty. We are thrilled beyond words when there comes restoration to our souls and spirits from His own gracious Spirit.

During my wife's illness and after her death I could not get over the strength, solace and serene outlook imparted to me virtually hour after hour by the presence of God's gracious Spirit Himself.

It was as if I was being repeatedly refreshed and restored, despite the most desperate circumstances all around me. Unless one has actually gone through such an experience it may seem difficult to believe. In fact there are those who claim they could not face such a situation. But for the man or woman who walks with God through these valleys, such real and actual refreshment *is* available.

The corollary to this is that only those

who have been through such dark valleys can console, comfort or encourage others in a similar situation. Often we pray or sing the hymn requesting God to make us an inspiration to someone else. We want, instinctively, to be a channel of blessing to other lives. The simple fact is that just as water can only flow in a ditch or channel or valley – so in the Christian's career, the life of God can only flow in blessing through the valleys that have been carved and cut into our own lives by excruciating experiences.

For example, the one best able to comfort another in bereavement is the person who himself has lost a loved one. The one who can best minister to a broken heart is one who has known a broken heart.

Most of us do not want valleys in our lives. We shrink from them with a sense of fear and foreboding. Yet in spite of our worst misgivings God can bring great benefit and lasting benediction to others through those valleys. Let us not always try to avoid the dark things, the distressing days. They may well prove to be the way of greatest refreshment to ourselves and those around us.

Philip Keller

The Spirit of the Lord is upon me, because
the Lord has anointed me to bring good
news to the suffering and afflicted. He has
sent me to comfort the broken-hearted, to
announce liberty to captives and to open the
eyes of the blind. He has sent me to tell
those who mourn that the time of God's
favour to them has come, and the day of his
wrath to their enemies. To all who mourn in
Israel He will give:

> Beauty for ashes;
> Joy instead of mourning;
> Praise instead of heaviness.

For God has planted them like strong and
graceful oaks for His own glory.

Isaiah 61:1–3

*Throughout the New Testament Jesus quotes verses
from the Old Testament, but this is so special
because Jesus reads this passage in the synagogue, as
quoted in Luke 4:18–19, and added 'These Scriptures
came true today!' What a statement! What a promise,
that as we believe and trust in Jesus He will give us
JOY instead of mourning.*

PART FOUR

The Cross

* * *

O Cross that liftest up my head,
I dare not ask to fly from thee;
I lay in dust life's glory dead,
And from the ground there blossoms red
Life that shall endless be.

Life is full of things we can't do anything about, but which we are supposed to do something with. 'He Himself endured the cross and thought nothing of its shame because of the joy.' A very different story from the one which would have been written if Jesus had been prompted by the spirit of our own age. 'Don't just endure the cross – *think* about it, talk about it, share it, express your gut-level feelings, get in touch with yourself, find out who you are, define the problem, analyse it, get counselling, get the experts' opinions, discuss solutions, work through it.' Jesus endured. He thought *nothing* of the shame. The freedom, the freshness of that valiant selflessness is like a strong wind. How badly such a wind is needed to sweep away the pollution of our self-preoccupation!

Elizabeth Elliot

PARABLES OF THE FOREST

Death of nursery days … happy sunlit hours of
    play.

Death of childhood dreams … when the reality
    of personal limitations overtakes fantasy.

Death of innocence … the first awareness of
    evil.

Death in leaving home … when separation
    registers.

Death in becoming a parent … when you
    become the care*taker*, rather than the
    receiver.

Death in the expectation of a perfect marriage.

Death in your child's first day of school …
    when the front door closes and silence
    grows heavy.

Death in the empty nest … when you no
    longer feel needed.

Death in the realisation that some expected
    goals will never be reached.

Death in the departure of friends … a nurturing
    source gone.

Death of freedom … when an incapacity
    confines an elderly loved one to your
    home.

Death in the awareness of aging … when mind
    and body won't respond as they once did.

Death in the wind up of working days … an
    identity lost.

Death in the end … that great enemy of health
    and youth.

But God says, 'Death is the gateway to life.'

It was at the Cross where Christ paid the
      penalty for sin.
It was through His death for us that God's gate
      to life opened.
Death shouted triumph ... for two days
But on the third day, resurrection
flung wide the doors of Eternal Life. What an
      incalculable gift for those accepting the
      death of another in their place!
For those refusing, the sentence of death
      remains Irreversible, Final.
But for those who enter it is a beginning not an
      ending.

Pamela Reeve

THE DONKEY

When fishes flew and forests walked
And figs grew upon thorn,
Some moment when the moon was blood
Then surely I was born;

With monstrous head and sickening cry
And ears like errant wings,
The devil's walking parody
On all four-footed things.

The tattered outlaw of the earth
Of ancient crooked will;
Starve, scourge, deride me: I am dumb,
I keep my secret still.

Fools! For I also had my hour;
One far fierce hour and sweet:
There was a shout about my ears,
And palms before my feet.

G. K. Chesterton

from
FACING THE STORM

Lord the donkey must have been surprised.
It wasn't used to all that noise.
It wasn't used to people riding on its back.
The flash of clothes
thrown down before its feet
was disconcerting.
Palm branches waving near its eyes,
off-putting.
The shouting of the crowd
incomprehensible.

And yet it seemed content to carry you.
I've seen no record of it rearing up,
or kicking.
It didn't seem to shy,
or back away.
Just plodded on,
the weight of God
light on its back.

I'm not like that.

I'll join the crowd,
cry blessings on you, Lord.
But, then, like them,
my welcome is conditional.
I like the thought
of your disturbing
other people's lives.
I'm with you, Lord,

in pointing out their faults,
and making your demands on them.
It's when you look at me
that I begin to get uncomfortable.

For, suddenly,
you take the tables of my life
and tip them upside down.
And all the things I hold so dear
go rolling down the aisles
of my hypocrisy.
Scattered and lost,
shown up for what they are,
or aren't.
And I stand there before you, empty.

All I can ask, Lord
Is that you'll put into my life
the same humility and willingness
the donkey had.
That bearing you
will be no heavy weight
your burden light
your yoke an easy fit.

Eddie Askew

We are pressed on every side by troubles but not crushed and broken. We are perplexed because we don't know why things happen as they do, but we don't give up. We are hunted down but God never abandons us. We get knocked down but we get up again and keep going.

These bodies of ours are constantly facing death just as Jesus did, so it is clear to all that it is only the living Christ *within* (who keeps us safe).

2 Corinthians 4:8–10

Jesus didn't come into the world to stop suffering, nor to explain it, nor to take it away, but to fill it with His presence.

Sent to Roy by a caring lady during his illness.

*C*harles Wesley wrote 9000 poems, of which 6500 were used as hymns, but he once said that he would gladly exchange them all for the privilege of writing this hymn.

> When I survey the wondrous cross
> On which the Prince of glory died,
> My richest gain I count but loss,
> And pour contempt on all my pride.
>
> Forbid it, Lord, that I should boast,
> Save in the death of Christ my God:
> All the vain things that charm me most,
> I sacrifice them to his blood.
>
> See from his head, his hands, his feet,
> Sorrow and love flow mingling down:
> Did e'er such love and sorrow meet,
> Or thorns compose so rich a crown?
>
> Were the whole realm of nature mine,
> That were an offering far too small,
> Love so amazing, so divine,
> Demands my soul, my life, my all.

Isaac Watts

*W*henever I sing this hymn it gives me a glorious sense of my own insignificance and causes me to focus on the One who through that 'wondrous cross' has brought meaning and reality to my life. I constantly have to remind myself that His love 'so amazing, so divine, demands my soul, my life, my all'.

The best rendition of this hymn that I have heard is Cliff Richard singing it unaccompanied. He graciously agreed to sing it at Roy's thanksgiving service in All Souls Church, Langham Place in November 1994.

FAITH

No coward soul is mine,
No trembler in the world's storm-troubled sphere.
I see Heaven's glories shine,
And Faith shines equal arming me from Fear.

O God within my breast,
Almighty, ever-present Deity!
Life – that in me has rest,
As I, Undying Life, have power in thee!

Vain are the thousand creeds
That move men's hearts – unutterably vain,
Worthless as withered weeds,
Or idlest froth amid the boundless main,

To waken doubt in one
Holding so fast by thine infinity;
So surely anchored on
The steadfast rock of Immortality.

With wide-embracing love
Thy spirit animates eternal years,
Pervades and broods above,
Changes, sustains, dissolves, creates, and rears.

Though earth and man were gone,
And suns and universes ceased to be,
And Thou were left alone,
Every Existence would exist in thee.

There is not room for Death,
Nor atom that his might could render void:
Thou – Thou art Being and Breath,
And what Thou art may never be destroyed.

Emily Brontë

After you have suffered a little while, our
God, who is full of kindness through Christ,
will give you his eternal glory. He personally
will come and pick you up, and set you
firmly in place, and make you stronger than
ever.

1 Peter 5:10

COME AND SEE

Come and see, come and see,
Come and see the King of love;
See the purple robe and crown of thorns He wears.
Soldiers mock, rulers sneer
As He lifts the cruel cross;
Lone and friendless now He climbs towards the
    hill.

We worship at your feet, where wrath and mercy
    meet,
And a guilty world is washed by love's pure stream.
For us He was made sin, oh, help me take it in.
Deep wounds of love cry out 'Father, forgive.'
I worship, I worship the Lamb who was slain.

Come and weep, come and mourn
For your sin that pierced Him there;
So much deeper than the wounds of thorn and
    nail.
All our pride, all our greed,
All our fallenness and shame;
And the Lord has laid the punishment on Him.

Man of heaven, born to earth
To restore us to Your heaven.
Here we bow in awe beneath Your searching eyes.
From Your tears come our joy.
From Your death our life shall spring:
By Your resurrection power we shall rise.

Graham Kendrick

I am a great fan of Graham Kendrick. His music and his lyrics are so sensitive and so appropriate. I wish this was a 'singing book' so that you could hear the beautiful plaintive melody which accompanies these words. You would not fail to be moved by the story of love that unfolds. As we worship we turn our eyes from ourselves and our problems towards 'the Lamb who was slain'.

O my Lord, when I think in how many ways Thou hast suffered, and that Thou didst in no wise deserve it, I do not know what to say for myself, nor of what I am thinking when I shrink from suffering, nor where I am when I excuse myself.... O Jesus, Thou brightest of eternal glory, solace of the pilgrim soul, with Thee is my mouth without voice and my silence speaks to Thee.

St Teresa of Avila and Thomas à Kempis

He nurses them when they are sick, and soothes their pains and worries.

In all their affliction he was afflicted, and he personally saved them. In his love and pity he redeemed them and lifted them up and carried them through all the years.

Sir, your good friend is very, very ill.

I am with you; that is all you need. My power shows up best in weak people.

I am glad to boast about how weak I am; I am glad to be a living demonstration of Christ's power, instead of showing off my own power and abilities.

I can do everything God asks me to with the help of Christ who gives me the strength and power.

Though our bodies are dying, our inner strength in the Lord is growing every day.

For in him we live and move and exist.

He gives power to the tired and worn out, and strength to the weak. Even the youths shall be exhausted, and the young men will all give up. But they that wait upon the Lord shall renew their strength. They shall mount up with wings like eagles; They shall run and not be weary; they shall walk and not faint.

The eternal God is your Refuge and underneath are the everlasting arms.

Ps 41:3; Is 63:9; Jn 11:3; 2 Cor 12:9; Phil 4:13; 2 Cor 4:16; Acts17:28; Is 40:29–31; Deut 33:27 (taken from Living Lights*)*

2 Corinthians 5:14–15 – Through suffering: Grieving our loss

We may be tempted to think that some lead an untroubled life. But in reality none of us bypasses difficulty and suffering. This, of course, is not to suggest that life metes this out equally. Nor are we suggesting that we all experience difficulty in the same way. We do not. Some are devastated by it and have to walk a very long road towards recovery. Others seem to be more resilient and bounce back with replenished optimism. But for both groups of people, the pressing question is: What can we learn from this experience?

Henri Nouwen suggests that 'finding new life through suffering and death: that is the good news.' Christ's death mirrors precisely that message. Suffering may seem senseless, but it need not have the last word. New hope can spring up from the ruins of previous expectations and plans. New life can come from the greatest disappointments.

But this can only come if we embrace the pain of our dashed hopes and grieve our loss to the point of relinquishment. It is at that place, with nothing in our hands, that good gifts will come our way.

Charles Ringma

Now may the Lord of peace Himself give you peace always in every way. The Lord be with you all.

2 Thessalonians 3:16

I talked to a man who was on the edge of experiencing the gift of a heart truly open to God. He had lost his twenty-five-year-old son. 'I'm really angry at God for doing this!' he said. 'How could he take this boy from me? He was a fine young man, believed in God, and had a great future. Now he's gone.'

The man had three problems: the loss of his beloved son and the grief that was causing, the anger he was feeling that was blocking him from receiving the only source of comfort, and he was belabouring false assumptions that this life is the best of all lives and that his son was being denied a long life. Most of all, the man was aching over the denial of his enjoyment of his son. Very human reactions. But beneath all the grief was a hardened, self-determining will that had been threatened. Though the man claimed to be a Christian, he had never yielded the core of his heart to the Lord.

The bright side of the story is that the Lord did not leave the man to muddle in his grief forever. I did all that I could to help him clarify his thinking about death and eternal life. One day I felt led to say, 'My friend, the Lord is going to give you a burning desire to open your heart to Him. He knows your grief. He gave His own Son to deal with the problem of death and to open heaven to us. I promise you that before long you will realise you can't make it without Him. That will open you to receive what He has been longing to give you. You are angry with God because you think He cancelled your plans.'

Some days later the man suddenly felt differently inside. He was gripped by an undeniable desire to surrender his grief and to confess how tenaciously he had held his own life and those he loved in his control. The Lord broke open the citadel of the man's heart and flooded it with His peace.

Lloyd Ogilvie

Once we have opened ourselves to grace, then Christ Himself takes up His dwelling in us. If we suffer, He suffers. We *are* His body here on earth. This poor human flesh, yours and mine, is where Jesus now lives, so pain bestows on us the incomprehensible privilege of helping to carry to completion the quota He must endure. As we accept this burden with thankfulness, we enter into an ever-deepening fellowship of His sufferings – but let us never forget that it was His own perfect and complete sacrifice of Himself that opened to us this possibility. Because of *that* we become His dwelling place. Ought not this to make us glad? Isn't this reason enough to make our sufferings a sacrifice of praise? ...

Abandonment to the Lord always *works* – not in the same way for everyone, of course. He deals with us according to His intimate knowledge of who we are and what we need to bring us into conformity with the image of His Son. It is conformity to that image that God is working on all the time, and what an encouragement to me it is to know that He is not going to give up on me until it is accomplished! *We shall be like Him.* That is His promise.

A spiritual outlook brings peace. 'Those who live on the level of our lower nature have their outlook formed by it, and that spells death; but those who live on the level of the spirit have the spiritual outlook, and that is life and peace … You are on the spiritual level, if only God's Spirit dwells within you; and if a man does not possess the Spirit of Christ, he is no Christian' (Rom 8:5–6,9).

Elizabeth Elliot

For whatever reason God chose to make man as he is – limited and suffering and subject to sorrows and death – He had the honesty and the courage to take His own medicine. Whatever game He is playing with His creation He has kept His own rules and played fair. He has Himself gone through the whole of human experience, from the trivial irritations of family life and lack of money to the worst horrors, pain, humiliation, defeat, despair and death. He was born in poverty and died in disgrace and felt it well worthwhile.

Dorothy L. Sayers

ONE SOLITARY LIFE

He was born in an obscure village. He worked in a carpenter shop until he was thirty. He then became an itinerant preacher. He never held an office. He never had a family or owned a house. He didn't go to college. He had no credentials but himself ...

Nineteen centuries have come and gone, and today he is the central figure of the human race. All the armies that ever marched, and all the navies that ever sailed, all the parliaments that ever sat, and all the kings that ever reigned have not affected the life of man on this earth as much as that ... One Solitary Life.

This next piece is quoted in a chapter on suffering in Stephen Gaukroger's book It Makes Sense. *It sums up very powerfully that we have a God who has experienced, and therefore understands, suffering.*

THE LONG SILENCE

At the end of time, billions of people were scattered on a great plain before God's throne. Most shrank back from the brilliant light before them. But some groups near the front talked heatedly – not with cringing shame but with belligerence. 'Can God judge us?'

'How can He know about suffering?' snapped a pert young brunette. She ripped open a sleeve to reveal a tattooed number from a Nazi concentration camp. 'We endured terror ... beating ... torture ... death!'

In another group a Negro boy lowered his collar. 'What about this?' he demanded, showing an ugly rope burn. 'Lynched for no crime but being black!'

In another crowd, a pregnant school girl with sullen eyes. 'Why should I suffer?' she murmured. 'It wasn't my fault.'

Far out across the plain were hundreds of such groups. Each had a complaint against God for the evil and suffering He permitted in His world. How lucky God was to live in heaven where all was sweetness and light, where there was no weeping or fear, no hunger or hatred. What did God know of all that men had been forced to endure in this world? For God leads a pretty sheltered life, they said.

So each of these groups sent forth their leader, chosen because he had suffered the most. A Jew, a Negro, a person from Hiroshima, a horribly deformed arthritic, a thalidomide child. In the centre of the plain they consulted with each other.

At last they were ready to present their case. It was rather clever. Before God could be qualified to be their judge, He must endure what they had endured. Their verdict was that God should be sentenced to live on earth – as a man! Let him be born a Jew. Let the legitimacy of his birth be doubted. Give Him a work so difficult that even His family will think Him out of His mind when He tries to do it. Let Him be betrayed by His closest friends. Let Him face false charges, be tried by a prejudiced jury and convicted by a cowardly judge. Let Him be tortured. At last, let Him see what it means to be terribly alone. Then let Him die. Let Him die so that there can be no doubt He died. Let there be a whole host of witnesses to verify it.

As each leader announced his portion of the sentence, loud murmurs of approval went up from the throng of people assembled. When the last had finished pronouncing sentence there was a long silence. No one uttered another word. No one moved. For suddenly all knew that God had already served His sentence.

Anon.

Our faith, then, is anchored not in signs and wonders but in the sovereign God of the universe. He will not 'perform' on cue to impress us. Jesus condemned those who wanted Him to put His miracles on display, saying, 'A wicked and adulterous generation asks for a miraculous sign! But none will be given it' (Matthew 12:39). He wants us to accept Him in the absence of proof. Jesus told Thomas, 'Blessed are those who have not seen and yet have believed' (John 20:29). We serve this Lord not because He dances to our tune, but because we trust His preeminence in our lives. Ultimately, He must be – He *will* be – the determiner of what is in our best interest. We can't see the future. We don't know His plan. We perceive only the small picture, and not even that very clearly. Given this limitation, it seems incredibly arrogant to tell God what to do – rather than making our needs known and then yielding to His divine purposes.

Jesus Himself modelled that attitude of submission for us. He asked His Father in the Garden of Gethsemane that the 'cup' of humiliation and death be removed from Him.

He knew fully what the crucifixion meant. The emotional pressure was so intense that great drops of blood penetrated His skin. Medically speaking, that phenomenon is called hematidrosis, and it occurs only in persons undergoing the most severe distress. Yet even in the midst of that agony, Jesus prayed, 'Yet not my will, but yours be done' (Luke 22:42).

James Dobson

Jesus' words in the Garden of Gethsemane have such powerful human meaning. Many a time we don't want to go through tough circumstances, but we have to yield ourselves into God's hands. Many times Roy paraphrased these words for himself. He would say, 'Well Lord, this isn't the way I would have chosen it, but if this is the way you want it, that's OK with me.' This is not trivialising Jesus' words, but submission to God's will for our lives and our circumstances.

There are many other biblical examples of this yielding to divine authority. The Apostle Paul asked the Lord on three separate occasions to remove the irritant he called 'a thorn in the flesh'. Three times the answer was no. Instead, he was told, 'My grace is sufficient for you, for my power is made perfect in weakness' (2 Corinthians 12:9).

James Dobson

In a similar way God led me to the words of Paul towards the end of Roy's life when I asked God if He was going to heal Roy. The answer came, 'No, but I am with you and that is all you need' (2 Corinthians 12:9).

Again, these examples of heartache illustrate the fact that godly people – praying people – sometimes face the same hardships that nonbelievers experience. If we deny that fact, we create even greater pain and disillusionment for those who are unprepared to handle it. That is why we must overcome our reluctance to admit these unpleasant realities. We must brace our brothers and sisters against the betrayal barrier. We must teach them not to depend too heavily on their own ability to comprehend the inexplicable circumstances in our lives.

Remember that the Scripture warns us to 'lean not on your own understanding' (Proverbs 3:5). Note that we are not prohibited from trying to understand. I've spent a lifetime attempting to get a handle on some of the imponderables of life, which has led to the writing of this book. But we are specifically told not to *lean* on our ability to make the pieces fit. 'Leaning' refers to the panicky demand for answers – throwing faith to the wind if a satisfactory response cannot be produced. It is pressing God to explain Himself – or else! That is where everything starts to unravel …

Admittedly, I do not have tidy answers that will satisfy [people who are suffering]. In fact, I find it irritating when amateur theologians throw around simplistic platitudes, such as 'God must have wanted a little flower for His heavenly garden.'

Nonsense! A loving Father does not tear the heart out of a family for selfish purposes! No, it is better to acknowledge that we have been given too few facts to explain all the heartache in an imperfect, fallen world. That understanding will have to await the coming of the sovereign Lord who promises to set straight all accounts and end all injustice.

James Dobson

Some years ago at our church we were challenged to commit ourselves afresh to God and to His service. These words remain a daily challenge to my life.

MY COVENANT WITH GOD

I take my stand before God today, and with honour and integrity declare that Jesus Christ is Lord of my life.

I now commit myself as far as I know how:

- to make Him Lord of my time, that I would use whatever days remain to me wisely and invest them for eternity.

- to make Him Lord of my gifts (both natural and spiritual), so that my life would have a new relevance in His service.

- to make Him Lord of my money – how I earn it, how I use it, how I save it, how I give it.

- to make Him Lord of my affections, so that I must be honourable before God in all my relationships.

Look up with wonder.
Look back with gratitude.
Look around with love.
Look within with honesty.
Look ahead with anticipation.

Jim Graham

Index of First Lines,
Titles and Authors

❋ ❋ ❋